You Can Draw
PEOPLE AT WORK

HB
HINKLER
BOOKS

Damien Toll

Introduction

Drawing is a fun and rewarding hobby for both children and adults alike. This book is designed to show how easy it is to draw great pictures by building them in simple stages.

What you will need

Only basic materials are required for effective drawing. These are:

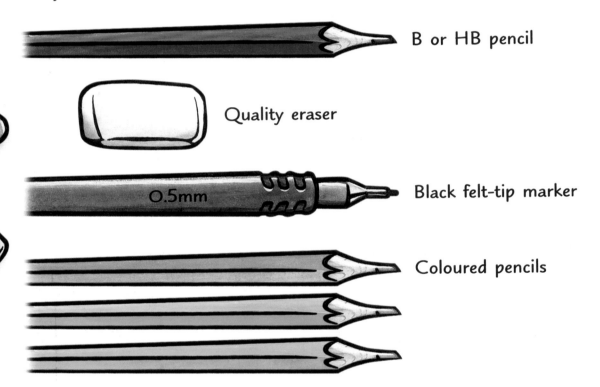

B or HB pencil

Quality eraser

0.5mm — Black felt-tip marker

Coloured pencils

These will be enough to get started. Avoid buying the cheapest pencils. Their leads often break off in the sharpener, even before they can be used. The leads are also generally too hard, making them difficult to see on the page.

Cheap erasers also cause problems by smudging rather than erasing. This often leaves a permanent stain on the paper. By spending a little more on art supplies in these areas, problems such as these can be avoided.

When purchasing a black marker, choose one to suit the size of your drawings. If you draw on a large scale, a thick felt-tip marker may be necessary. If you draw on a medium scale, a medium-point marker will do and if on a small scale, a 0.3mm, 0.5mm, 0.7mm or 0.8mm felt-tip marker will best suit.

The stages

Simply follow the lines drawn in orange on each stage using your B or HB pencil. The blue lines on each stage show what has already been drawn in the previous stages.

1.

2.

3.

In the final stage the drawing has been outlined in black and the simple shape and wire-frame lines erased. The shapes are only there to help us build the picture. We finish the picture by drawing over the parts we need to make it look like our subject with the black marker, and then erasing all the simple shape lines.

4.

Included here is a sketch of a builder as it would be originally drawn by an artist.

These are how all the people in this book were originally worked out and drawn. The orange and blue stages you see above are just a simplified version of this process. The drawing here has been made by many quick pencil strokes working over each other to make the line curve smoothly. It does not matter how messy it is as long as the artist knows the general direction of the line to follow with the black marker at the end. The pencil lines are erased and a clean outline is left. Therefore, do not be afraid to make a little mess with your B or HB pencil, as long as you do not press so hard that you cannot erase it afterwards.

Grids made of squares are set behind each stage in this book. Make sure to draw a grid lightly on your page so it does not press into the paper and show up after being erased. Artist tips have also been added to show you some simple things that can make your drawing look great. Have fun!

Olympian

Almost everyone has dreamt of being an Olympic athlete. Being the best in the world at something is a major achievement. Olympians have to practise for a long time, often starting very young. When they are old enough, they can participate in the Olympic Games. The Olympics are held every four years. Each time, a different country hosts the event.

1.

Begin by drawing a grid with three equal squares going across and down.

Draw the shapes for his head, hair and neck, in the correct position on the grid.

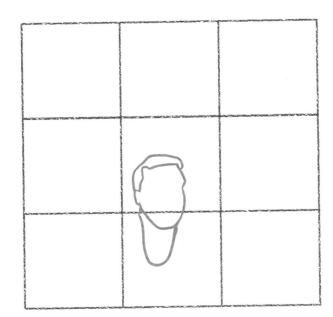

2.

Draw in his muscly shoulders and part of his arms.

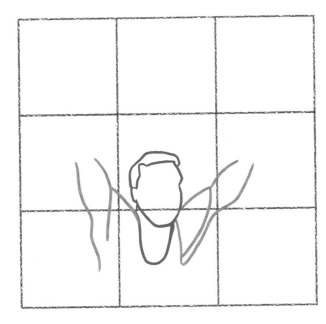

3.

Add his forearms and hands. Draw in his singlet. Notice how short it looks here. Most of it is bent under, so we do not see it.

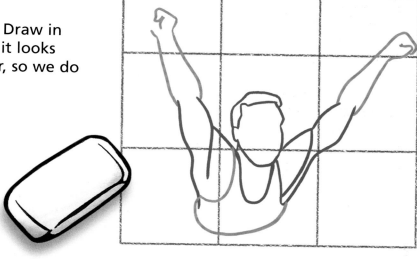

4.

Draw his legs and shoes. Notice how few lines are needed to make up these. Sometimes we make things too complicated when they are really simple. Add the rings and his fingers around the rings. Finish with his facial features.

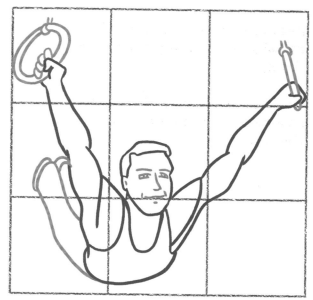

5.

Outline and colour your Olympian. You may like to put your own country's Olympic colours on his outfit.

Musician

Musicians play many different types of instruments. They travel from place to place, writing and performing new songs about their beliefs or aspirations. Many musicians sing, but you don't need to have a good voice to be a musician. Musicians have a talent for playing their instrument and this talent comes from lots and lots of practice.

1.

Begin by drawing a grid with three equal squares going across and down.

Draw in the shapes for the hair and the head at the top and middle of the grid.

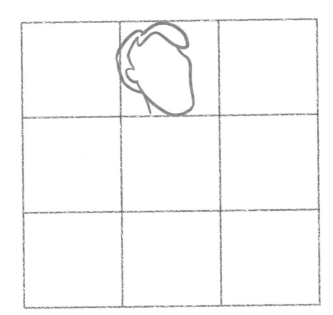

2.

Draw in the facial features. Add the shoulders and the arm. Draw in the shirt sleeves.

3.

Draw some music notes around his mouth. Draw in the guitar.

4.

Add the hand that's curved around the guitar and the trousers underneath.

5.

Outline and colour in your drawing. Musicians don't wear any specific coloured clothes so you could colour him in any way you like.

Firefighter

Firefighters are there to help protect the community. As soon as they hear of a fire, they put on their uniform and race to the scene. Firefighters don't only extinguish fires, they also help out in other emergencies, like when a cat is stuck up a tree or a car accident has happened.

1.

Begin by drawing a grid with three equal squares going across and down.

Draw in the firefighter's hat and the outline of his face. Draw in the collar of his coat and his arm.

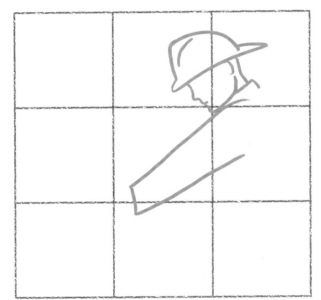

2.

Add the shape for his hand and the fire hydrant. Draw in his other arm and the bottom of his collar.

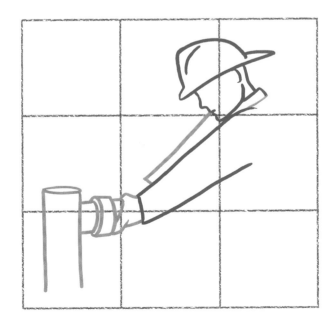

3.

Finish off the details for the hydrant. Draw a long curved line for his back. Draw in his leg and shoe.

4.

Add in his eye and his hair. Draw the line for the inside of his ear. Add the reflective stripes on his jacket. Draw in his other leg and shoe with his knee on the ground.

5.

Outline your drawing and colour it in.

Chef

Chefs are the masters of the kitchen. They make food taste, look, feel and smell great. They speedily prepare meals that are of superb quality. Sometimes a chef will spend a lot of time trying to work out a perfect combination of ingredients that will taste fantastic.

1.

Begin by drawing a grid with three equal squares going across and down.

Draw in the rounded shape for the chin and ear. Draw in the shape for the chest and stomach.

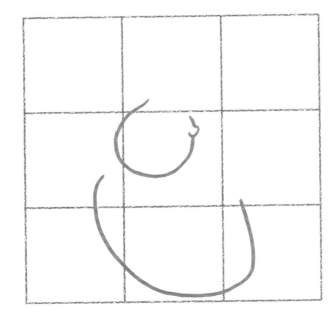

2.

Add the chef's facial features and hat. Draw in his arms. Finish with his coat buttons.

3.

Add the chef's puffy hat top. Draw in the hands and the big spoon.

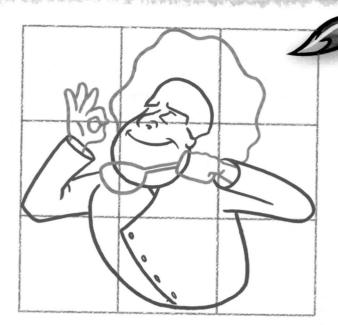

4.

Define the hand with the spoon in it with lines for fingers. Draw in the steam lines to finish.

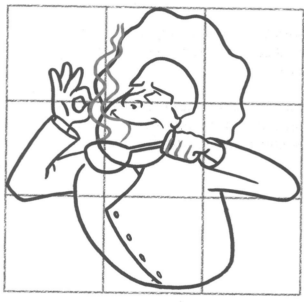

5.

Because chefs wear white, we can use shading to colour his clothes. Notice that shadows will appear on the underside of things because the light is blocked from the top.

Builder

Builders make everything from large skyscrapers to the houses we live in. They use many different tools to cut, drill and measure many pieces that fit together to make up a structure. They also organise teams of tradespeople for their project. Builders get up early in the morning so they can get a full day's work in. Building can often be hard work.

1.

Begin by drawing a grid with three equal squares going across and down.

Draw a circle for his protective hat. Add a line around it for the peak. Draw in the shape of his face and neck.

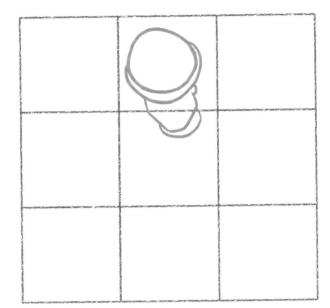

2.

Add the eyes, nose and mouth. Draw in the t-shirt and arms. Notice the position of the hands.

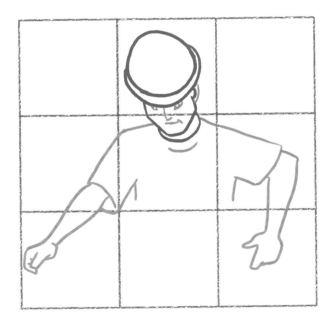

3.

Draw the curved lines for the middle of his hat. Draw his overalls over his t-shirt. Add a curve at his left hand for the tape-measure and a long line going to his right hand. Draw in the lines for the long piece of timber.

4.

Draw his tool belt around his waist. You may like to add some tools of your own.

5.

Colour in your builder. Notice how there are some wavy lines on the timber to make it look like wood grain.

Camera Man

The camera man operates the video camera, trying to get the best view of the action to interest the viewer at home. Sometimes they have to have a lot of patience, especially when filming children and animals, because they can be unpredictable.

1.

Begin by drawing a grid with three equal squares going across and down.

Next, draw some circles for the lens. Make sure they are in the correct position on the grid.

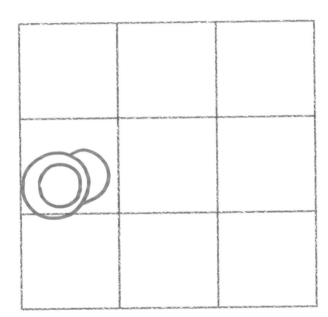

2.

Draw the camera around the lens.

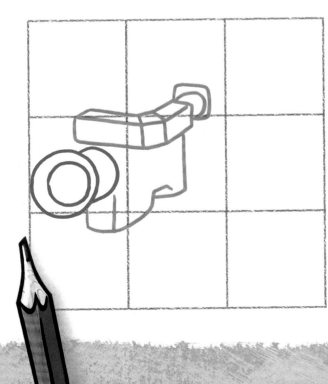

3.

Draw the shape for the hand at the front of the camera. Add the microphone on the side and the handle at the back. Draw in the shapes for the man's head and hair.

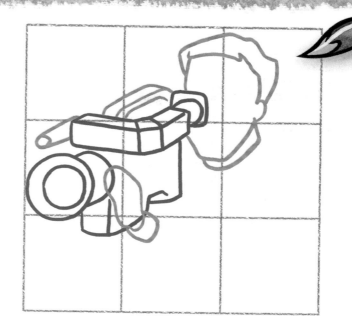

4.

Draw the facial features. Add some lines to separate the hand into fingers. Draw in his jacket.

5.

Colour in your camera man to finish. Notice how the camera is black, but not totally black. This is because even black reflects light and in turn appears light or grey in parts.

Vet

Vets are like doctors for your pets. They check your dog's pulse or your cat's temperature and give them medicine if they are sick. Vets know a lot about animals, how they behave and where all their organs are. Sometimes if your pet is really sick the vet comes to you. Vets really like animals.

1.

Begin by drawing a grid with four equal squares going across and three down.

Draw in the shapes for the vet's head and hair. Draw the shape for the dog's head and ear.

2.

Add her facial features and the top of her coat. Draw in the dog's tongue and his eyes and nose. Draw the vet's hand and coat sleeve above the dog's head.

3.

Draw the dog's other ear, joining up to the vet's hand shape. Add a curved line for her shirt under her chin. Draw in the lines for the table top. Add the vet's arm and hand shape. Draw the shape for the dog's body to finish this stage.

4.

Define the hands with lines for the fingers. Add the highlight points in the dog's eyes and nose. Draw the dog's legs and tail to finish.

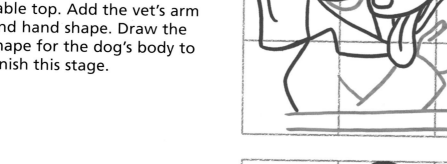

5.

Outline and colour in your drawing. The vet's coat is white, so to make her stand out better the background is coloured grey.

Tennis Player

Tennis players are athletes. They train really hard to be the best they can. When a player gets to the professional stage, they will travel all over the world. They will play tennis against other competitors and try to win various competitions. Tennis is a fun game to play with your friends.

1.

Begin by drawing a grid with three equal squares going across and down.

Draw in the wire-frame with shapes for the head and hands. Add the shoes.

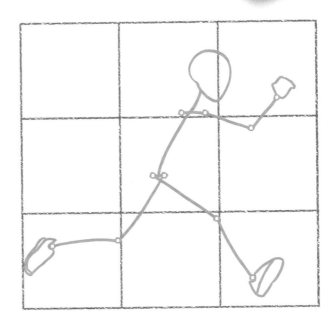

2.

Draw in the shape for the body and the tennis racquet. Draw a small circle for the ball.

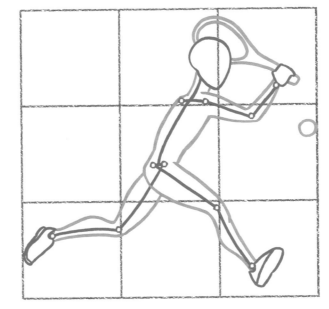

3.

Draw her clothes over the top of her body. Add the details for her face and hair. Draw in the criss-crossed lines for the racquet strings. Put in some curved lines for her socks to finish.

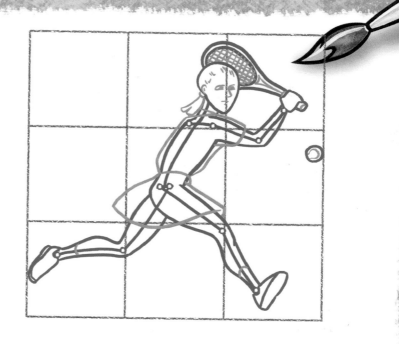

Artist Tip:

The orange lines on this girl are called 'wire-frames'. These wire-frames are a simplified version of a skeleton. The lines represent the bones and the circles represent the joints. If we can understand the size of the parts of the skeleton and how it moves, we can build our subject around it and it will look natural. There are often three stages to this. Look at the tennis player stages in this book and you will see the skeleton is drawn first, followed by the body and then the clothes over the top.

4.

Outline your drawing and colour it in. Tennis players wear many different outfits. You make like to try different colour combinations and even design your own clothes.

Doctor & Nurse

Doctors are there to help us get well when we are sick. They know a lot about how our body works, so if something goes wrong they know the best way to fix it. Nurses help the doctor take care of us when we're in hospital. They check on you every so often to make sure everything is going okay.

1.

Begin by drawing a grid with three equal squares going across and down.

Draw in the rectangular shape for the clipboard. Draw in the shapes for the doctor's body, arms, head and hair.

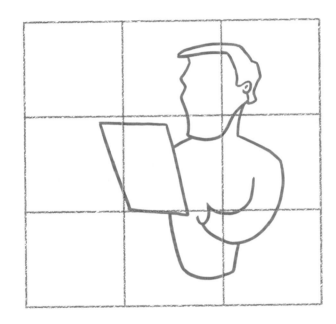

2.

Add the mirror on top of his head. Draw in his facial features and the stethescope around his neck. Add the hand holding onto the clipboard, his legs and his shoes. Draw a line down the middle for his coat.

3.

Draw the collar for his coat. Draw in the nurse, paying close attention to the the point where she intersects the grid lines.

4.

Add her hat and her mischievous facial features. Finish by drawing in the syringe.

5.

Outline and colour your doctor and nurse.

Policeman

The police have a very important role in our society. Their main job is to maintain order, fight crime and patrol the neighbourhood to make sure everyone is safe. Sometimes they do other jobs, like direct traffic. You're not allowed to have a criminal record if you want to become a policeman.

1.

Begin by drawing a grid with three equal squares going across and down.

Draw in the shape for the cheeks, small ear and hat peak. Add his mouth and the lines for his shoulders.

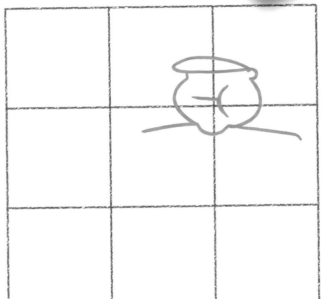

2.

Draw in his hat. Add half-circle curves under the peak of his hat for his eyes. Draw in a zig-zag line for some hair. Add his long, curved arms and body.

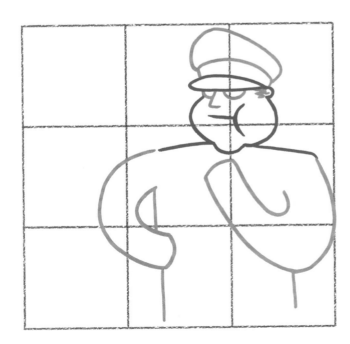

3.

Draw the police symbol on his hat. Draw the lines for the checkered pattern on his hat. Add his collar and his hand holding the whistle. Draw in his other hands with the movement marks. Finish with the buttons and coat line.

Artist Tip:

Drawings, like photos, are still pictures. They cannot move. We can, however, portray movement by drawing lots of the same thing. Here we have drawn three right hands. This shows he is moving it very quickly. This is further shown in the arcs highlighted by the dotted lines. These arcs are lightly coloured with the same colour as where his hand and clothes have been. Try waving your hand quickly in front of your face to see the arc and how many hands you can count.

4.

Outline your drawing and colour it in. This policeman is wearing a blue uniform but some policemen wear black.

Astronaut

Astronauts get to pilot big spaceships and dress up in space suits. Some even get to go to the moon. They have to go through lots of training to be prepared, in case anything goes wrong when they are in space. The astronaut you're about to draw is holding a really heavy weight, because on the moon there isn't as much gravity so things don't seem to weigh much at all.

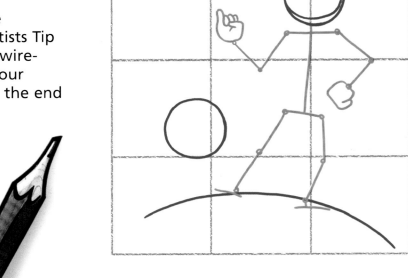

1.

Begin by drawing a grid with three equal squares going across and down.

Continue by drawing the circles for the helmet high on the right side of the grid. Notice the circle inside the helmet is slightly squashed. Draw another circle for the Earth and a big arc at the bottom for the moon.

2.

Draw the wire-frame for the astronaut's body (see the Artists Tip for the tennis player about 'wire-frames'). This is the basis of our character. Draw his hands at the end of these.

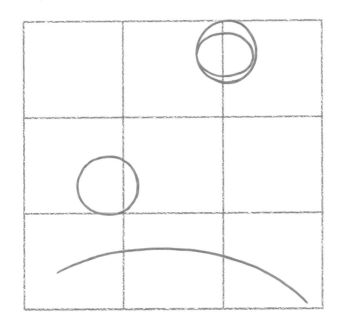

3.

Add the space suit over the wire-frame making it fairly puffy. Draw in the panels on his torso.

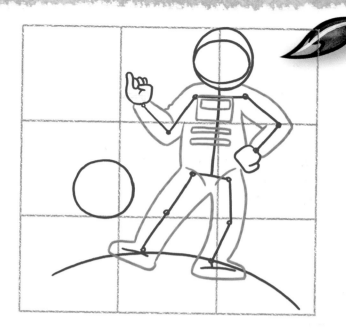

4.

Draw the barbell on top of his finger. Draw the face inside the helmet. Add some lines for his backpack. Draw in the clouds and countries on the Earth and the craters on the moon.

5.

Outline and colour in. You can colour the background black and use dabs of white paint or correction pen for the stars. Here we have put a shadow under him to show he is slightly off the face of the moon. This highlights the weightlessness.

Artist

An artist spends lots of time creating their art work. They understand what colours look the best together and creatively arrange them in some sort of picture to look amazing. A typical artist has an easel on which they paint or draw. Some artists don't become famous until long after they have died.

1.

Begin by drawing a grid with three equal squares going across and down.

First draw the peanut-like shape for the head. Add the curved lines for the arms and hand. Finish this stage by drawing in the rest of the body. Check that everything is in the correct position on the grid.

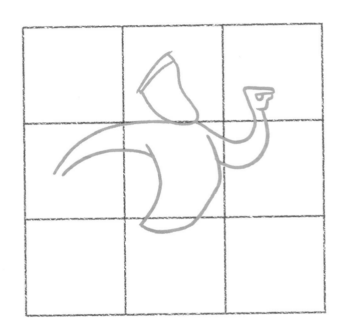

2.

Draw the hat on top of the head shape. Draw the skewed rectangle shape for his canvas. Add a shape for the hand. Draw an arc for the legs. Make sure they go from being thin at the bottom to thicker at the top.

3.

Draw in the facial features. Separate the hand shape with lines for the fingers. Draw the legs for the easel.

4.

Draw some hair coming out from under his hat. Add the moustache. Draw the paint brush in his hand and finish with the rest of the lines for the easel.

5.

Outline your drawing and colour it in. You can make the artist's clothes any colour you like. Don't forget to draw in a work of art on the easel!

Office Worker

Office workers sit at a desk all day, filling out seemingly endless amounts of paperwork. Often when things don't work people get really stressed. Computers crashing, your boss asking you to work late, too many phones ringing, coffee supplies running out and a paper cut are all typical events that can happen on an average day's work at the office.

1.

Begin by drawing a grid with three equal squares going across and down.

Then draw a line for the eyes. Draw the half-circle eyes and the nose under this line. Draw in the warped computer screen.

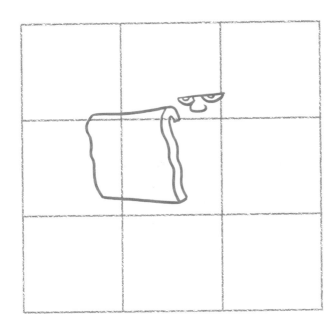

2.

Add the head shape around the eyes. Draw in the collar and top of the tie. To finish this stage, draw in the stack of papers next to the screen and the back parts of the screen.

3.

Draw in the shape for the mouth and the teeth. Draw the arm with the shoulder above the neck. Draw in the bit for the other shoulder. Add the rest of the tie. Draw in the desk.

4.

Draw some steam lines above the head. Add some steam coming out of the ears. Add the wrinkles, eyebrows and hair. Draw a shape to show the computer steaming and some dreary eyes on the back of the screen. Draw some paper on the desk and the guy's hand. Draw some lines to define the paper stack.

5.

Outline your drawing. We have made his face red to show how mad he's getting.

Soldier

The army is made up of soldiers. Soldiers are disciplined and train really hard. They are ordered to have short hair and be clean-shaven. They get woken up by a bugle early in the morning and get prepared for another day's training. Sometimes they have to go to war to protect people.

1.

Begin by drawing a grid with three equal squares going across and down.

Now draw a wire-frame with the hand and face shapes on the correct position on the grid.

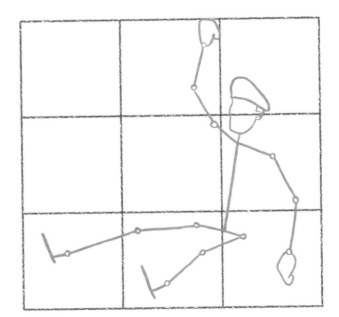

2.

Here we draw on the body around the wire-frame. This is explained in the Artist Tip on the tennis player page.

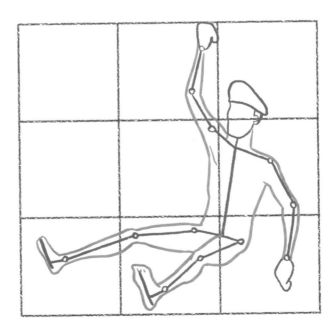

3.

The clothes are then drawn fitting loosely over the body. Clothes are generally bigger than the body.

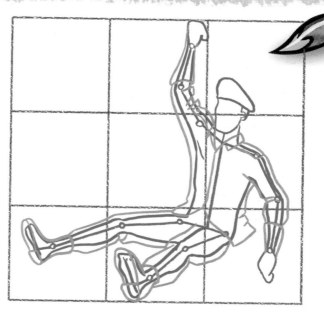

4.

The details are added last. When we outline our drawing, we do not need to draw in the wire-frame or his body underneath his clothes because we cannot see them.

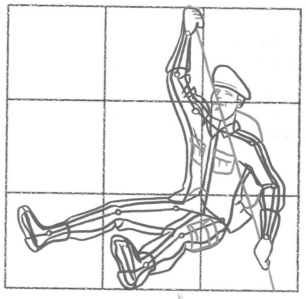

5.

If you have followed the steps correctly, you have just drawn the soldier exactly the same way a comic book artist draws his figures.

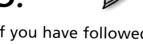

Check out these great titles in the *You Can Draw* series!

Learn how to draw all sorts of wild animals, pets, farm animals, sea creatures, insects, cartoon characters, people at work and cars.

Published in 2005 by
Hinkler Books Pty Ltd
45-55 Fairchild Street
Heatherton Victoria 3202 Australia

© Hinkler Books Pty Ltd 2005
Written and illustrated by Damien Toll
With thanks to Jared Gow
10 9 8 7 6 5
10 09 08

ISBN : 978 1 7415 7176 9
Printed and bound in Malaysia